DRAG QUEENS I

This book is dedicated to the wild, wonderful and mysterious creature called the

Drag Queen.

Queens - radiating deep, divine feminine nature, who are never afraid to be too much! Mocking the stereotypes, pushing the limits, rekindling the fairy-tales!

We love 'em. We envy 'em. We just can't live without 'em!

Enjoy these coloring pages. Please leave a review.
and share your ideas for future coloring books.

Check out CatandCrowDesign.com for free coloring pages,
downloads and giveaways

xox

cat and crow design
SOULFULLY SOURCED

Acid Betty
Aja
Alaska Thunderfuck
Alyssa Edwards
Anka Shayne
ANNA REXIA
Aquaria
BOB
Coco Peru
Dame Edna
DESMOND NAPOLES
DETOX
Divine
Raven
Kim Chi
Jackie Beat
Jiggly Caliente
Jinx Monsoon
Porcelain
Lactatia
LATRICE ROYALE
Lee Fontaine
Martha Graham Cracker
Mathu Andersen
MILK
Miss Fame
Naomi Smalls
Piper D'Bulge
Quentin Crisp
Tammy Brown
RAJA GEMINI
Trinity Taylor
Russell Alldread
SHARON NEEDLES
STACY LAYNE MATTHEWS
Violet Chachki

this page intentionally left blank

Acid Betty

this page intentionally left blank

Alaska
Thunderfuck

Alyssa Edwards

Anka Shayne

ANNA REXIA

this page intentionally left blank

Aquaria

BOB
I GET UP OUT OF BED
I PUT ON MY CLOTHES
'CAUSE I GOT
BILLS TO
PAY

Coco
Peru

this page intentionally left blank

Dame Edna

this page intentionally left blank

DESMOND NAPOLES

DETOX

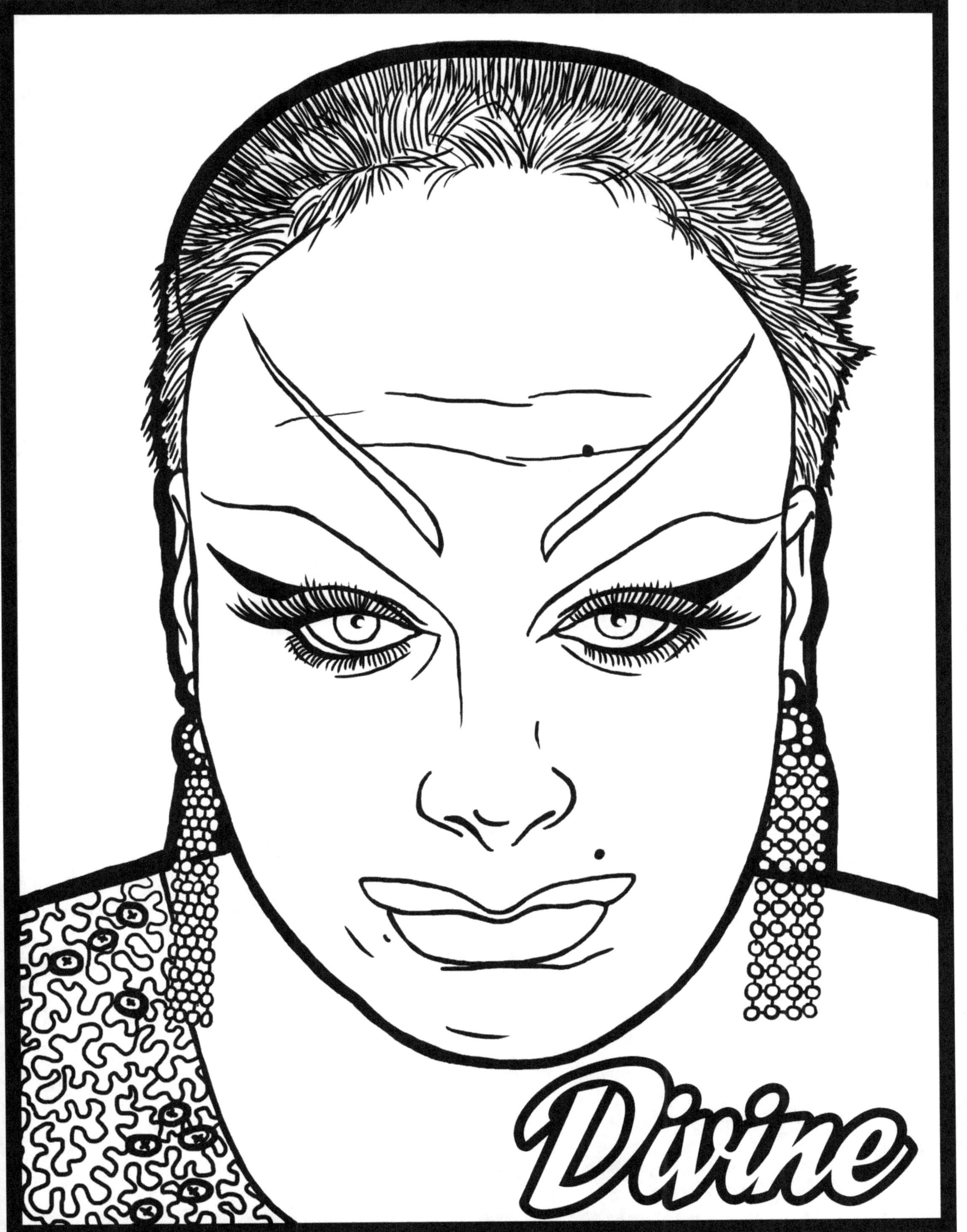

Divine

this page intentionally left blank

Ginger Minj

Jackie Beat

this page intentionally left blank

Jiggly Caliente

Jinx Monsoon

KimChi

Lactatia

this page intentionally left blank

LATRICE ROYALE

this page intentionally left blank

Lee Fontaine

this page intentionally left blank

Martha Graham Cracker

this page intentionally left blank

Mathu Andersen

MILK

Miss Fame

this page intentionally left blank

Naomi Smalls

this page intentionally left blank

Piper D'Bulge

Quentin Crisp

Raven

RAJA GEMINI

this page intentionally left blank

Trinity Taylor

Russell Alldread

SHARON NEEDLES

STACY LAYNE MATTHEWS

this page intentionally left blank

Porcelain

Tammy Brown

Violet Chachki

this page intentionally left blank